THE

SUTRAS

OF

UNSPEAKABLE

JOY

THE

SUTRAS

OF

UNSPEAKABLE

JOY

MEGGAN WATTERSON

Artwork by Lisbeth Cheever-Gessaman
(She Who Is)

"Duende" p.viii, "Magdalena" p.14, "Lilith" p.20, "Coniunctio"
p.32, "Love's Secret" p.38, "Night and Her Train of Stars" p.46,
"Ascent of the White Queen" p.60, "Union of the Divine" p.72,
"The Cosmic Egg" p.78.

MEGGAN WATTERSON, LLC
ISBN-13: 978-0692681169 (Custom Universal)
ISBN-10: 0692681167

:::AN INTRODUCTION:::

Here's why I wrote this little book of love poems.

What I have wanted most in this life is a love that will never leave. And I realized that maybe I hadn't met with a love like that outside of me, in someone else, because I hadn't met an unfaltering love from within me. So I decided I would retreat for 40 days with my red pen to try to tether together the small-ego-everyday-me to the me that's a lighthouse-type-of-soul, the me that's just undiluted love. I wanted to anchor once and for all into the love that's within me, to a love that could never leave because it's the truth of who I am. Whether I'm with a partner or alone, I wanted to feel free- entirely my own- an Ouroboros whose love circles back into herself.

This book is one-part sutras, one-part love poems, and one-part psychic twine. They tell my whole truth. They reveal my ardor for the divine. They unite the masculine, manly aspects of me with the womanly, feminine aspects of me that I have sought to balance. They reconcile body and soul, human and divine, animal and angel, light and the dark, or basically- all that we can be conscious of containing.

What I didn't realize until after I wrote this book is that there's an ancient Tantric text called the Vijnana Bhairava Tantra, which is translated as something like "the terror and joy of realizing oneness with the soul." It contains a poetic dialogue between the divine feminine and the divine masculine, between Shiva and Shakti, but in the case of this book it's more like a sacred back and forth between Jesus Christ and Mary Magdalene.

Ultimately, this book is a collection of love letters to and from my own soul.

The Sutras of Unspeakable Joy are the 40 days I devoted to ending a pattern of thinking that love, true and unwavering, was something I would meet outside of me. It's a poetic conversation between the side of me that keeps forgetting that the deepest source of love comes from the divine and can only be met from within. And that side of me that is that love, completely, utterly, fully.

And what I did by devoting these 40 days to trying with words to realize oneness with the soul- is that I embodied the truth I have always taught. That love is what we are, not what we find- that true love is here-within us. And, that no cathedral can ever compare to the massive spirit in the messy sinews of this human heart.

:::AN INVOCATION:::

Initiation

Falling in love is an initiation,
our most ancient rite.
It's the cult we all belong to.
It's a labyrinth we get thrown in, blindfolded.
We want to know the way through.
We want, often desperately, to be told which way to turn,
when to stop,
when to take that next step forward.
But the nature of initiation is that it exacts what's new.
We can't move in those well tread ways we're used to,
we can't depend on those very patterns
that led us here: in love.
And the Minotaur offers no solace.
He has no husky-voiced revelations to lend us in the dark.
He's hard-wired with his horned-head to destroy, to devour.
He's that impulse, that compulsion in so
many of us to tear apart the possibility of
rebirth. He's to be expected, not feared.
He's that ferociously unconscious
beast we all have to sacrifice.
I'm not the slaying type like Theseus.
But every cell in me was made for surrender.
So I will sacrifice my fear of where love is leading me.
And I will surrender to the bone-knowing I possess
that love comes to us as an answered prayer.

ONE

We met in a place just beyond where words can reach.
Writing ends where the body's body begins.
A dark reckoning of a deeper knowing.
In the beginning was not the word.
The word is birthed from what my
body knows sovereign to light.
The body is that silence that knows itself completely.
And in that silence you knew me.

TWO

It's that I want to feel you always.
And yet become convinced that it's you who does the leaving,
when like this morning I awake alone.
I confuse my own inconsistency as yours.
I forget that I was the one who stayed up all night
securing this turret around my heart.
You never ask for an apology or an explanation.
You just reach out through the space I've created
and offer me your hand.

THREE

You ask nothing of me.
There's no proof, no condition,
no evidence of my worth needed.
You love me because I exhale.
Because I exist.
Because I came back for you.
And to love you in return,
all I have to do is love the world.

FOUR

I am a solitary resolve.
It is all I have ever been.
I have no use for the concept of the holy,
for pure things,
for an ideal of the faithful.
I am only what must be done to be with you.

FIVE

Triumph is remembering,
closer and closer to when I've forgotten,
the beauty of what it feels like to know you.

SIX

It takes many words to get to the real words,
to the truth that is as true as a bare white bone in the dirt.
The moon last night wouldn't let me rest,
until I could say you in one sentence.
Until I could feel you invoked with these words:
You are the love that remains.

SEVEN

There's a boat made of alabaster waiting
for me when I close my eyes.
I know I'm meant to unmoor the anchor.
I know I'm meant to climb inside,
and trust the slow, dark waters to carry me.
I feel you whisper the courage I need,
caress my cheek, kiss the top of my hand.
So that, as I stand on this edge of everything I once was,
I am baptized by the promise of your love.

EIGHT

The angels are impotent without our human faith.
The ardor it takes to believe something so faint,
so dulcet and unsteady as whispered light in the depths.
In my story it took the form of an egg,
the ovum philosophicum, the sacred vessel.
The gilded essence of who I am;
the dark womb that gives birth to gold.
In the sanctuary of my heart long before I met you,
I heard that you would give me back my name,
that one morning our love would return us to life.
And that in this moment of recognition
Of hearing my name in your voice,
our ministry would begin, and that together,
we would resurrect into the love that never changes.

NINE

Love is the force that renders us all equal.
The other is the self; there is no separation.
Eye to eye, every man, woman, animal and angel,
we are all aching toward the light.
More than the stability of hearth and home,
I have always wanted to be my own.
To love and be loved from a place of freedom,
a love without possession or addiction,
a love that is more than love.
This is what I live for: to source my own love from within.
To ready your arrival, beloved,
in this field, this expanse of my well lit heart.

TEN

I haven't exhaled once without also calling your name.
This quiet secret behind my eyes,
this inviolable desire to be with you,
moves me through the arch of each day-
my consolation, my companion in place of you.
And I thought I understood, I thought I knew.
But last night, your words confused me,
made me cry so hard I laughed.
It's the start of something new.
A question that forced my heart into flames:
"Why have you kept me from you?"

ELEVEN

This is what I've come here to tell you.
I am done with tormented, with half-in,
with a love that lacks hands and feet.
I am done with the thought that I could drown,
with fear that this light could burn out,
with forgetting that I was brought here to rise.
I am done with these long nights, with this unlived desire,
with this disbelief that I could be fully loved.
I am done with being left, beloved,
so I vow to be the one to never leave you.

TWELVE

There is a place no one else can reach except you.
It's how I feel you with me.
That inner-most-place is suddenly no longer empty.
And the angels swoon each time I remember:
you never leave, you never arrive.
You are this love that abides.
You are what I open myself up to from within.
I brace then for the impact of honey in my bloodstream,
for what flesh feels like when it turns to gold.

THIRTEEN

Loving you has taken me through everything.
All my illusions of you are limp on the floor.
I didn't realize the heart could break so gratefully.
I didn't realize the heart can only ever expand.
I didn't realize that here at this depth,
in this darkness, this place of solid ash,
you live like a quiet pulse,
like a diamond beneath the earth of
what I can't understand.
You live on the other side of humility, of broken, of alone.
Once I can let go of every story that got me here.
Once my self is impossibly small, beloved,
this is when you radiate out through me, my every pore.

FOURTEEN

I want what's timeless to inhabit my bones.
Surrender is the only gatekeeper.
It's all that is ever asked of me,
to fall inward, to trust that voice that comes,
when I'm leveled again by a desire so singular.
For this love to reach where it has never been before.
For this love to hand me back this truth-
that I am nothing more than the albino peacock
of my own incandescent soul.

FIFTEEN

It's not your name, it's how I feel when I say it.
It compels me to exist more intensely.
Right here in this odd mix of soul and breath,
it calls me back from all times and all places.
So I am nowhere else but with you.
This is the home you make of my blood and body.
Every time I say your name I am claimed, I belong.
I am what I came here to be: beloved.

SIXTEEN

Love is the effort of the soul becoming real.
It's the hard-won practice of just being fully here.
Love is the vow I make when I've lived to the end of fear,
when all of my excuses have lost their currency.
When I am ready to hold, and do no harm.
When I am willing to become what seeks to unify,
even in the darkest night, and deepest pain, I do not leave.
Because love is the memory that I am you.
That wherever I go, beloved, I cannot be lost to you.

SEVENTEEN

I write in red because of you.
Every word is a breadcrumb,
to find my way back to when I first met you.
I couldn't speak or move.
My hands were pressed together in prayer,
something I had never seen them do.
I looked up with eyes closed,
I wanted to stay as still as I could,
to meet your presence within me.
You were everywhere, especially in my bloodstream.
My existence had never wanted to be so singular,
so focused on all that has ever mattered.
I could feel the pulse in my exposed neck,
arched and dove white like an offering.
This was the day you claimed me.
This is the cathedral I have never left.

EIGHTEEN

I understand the necessity of the labyrinth,
the minotaur, the fleur-de-lis with its golden flames,
the idea of the darkness, of being lost,
the metaphor of the seven gates, of having
to get naked deep underground.
I understand the necessity of the trials, the obstacles,
of testing the seeker's resolve, of the purity
it takes to tame the unicorn.
I understand that there are no certainties I'll see the light.
And so I've done what all this is meant to do.
I've become so intimate with fear,
I am now the presence that exists at the end of it.

NINETEEN

There were so many nights when I doubted.
So many times I feared a wrong move,
as if I could go where you wouldn't be.
As if you weren't already with me as I searched for you.
I've misunderstood that dream you gave me years ago.
I thought it was a taste of what heaven
feels like here on earth.
I thought it was predictive, a vision of what's to come.
I feared that I would never find that bliss again.
But the dream was revelatory; it was
a reflection of my own soul.
You wanted me to feel how this love is unlike any other.
You wanted me to feel physically the energy of our union.
Not to charge me with the weight of finding it,
but to let me experience the truth
that I can never take a step that isn't toward you.

TWENTY

In the silence of what I thought I knew,
you remind me that the heart is not a heart.
And that my body has never been mine alone.
The heart is a diamond, an ever-expanding mansion,
with a single door left unlocked for you.
Humility brings me to the threshold.
But it's the body's joy that carries me through.
The body isn't a body but structured light,
faceted just right to appear fleeting, mortal, momentary.
But there's joy in the body that's eternal.
And the genesis of that joy is when I see you seeing me.
The alchemy of this turns my spine into love's own frame.
And the honey love is seeps not from
your beloved body or mine
but from the marrow of us both
from our once shared body, our once shared bone.

TWENTY-ONE

It only gets lighter.
After the darkest dark,
after my tender feet have touched the earth
beneath the ocean I feel for you,
I ascend with the depths in my eyes.
Because loving you is just the start.
I'm the one who must weld this union from within.
I'm the one who must stand bravely on
the bridge between the worlds,
and receive all that I have ever asked for.
I'm the one who has to trust again
that my hands are your own,
that I have never in my life worked alone.
That together we become what I came here to
share: the love that is love that is love.

TWENTY-TWO

I don't need much, beloved. Really.
All I need is the focus of your irises,
on this lionhearted effort I'm making
to dismantle those unseen barriers
that support the illusion you're apart from me.
All I need is a clear expanse,
a field that's unfettered by the laws of logic.
A harbor. A sanctuary.
A place I can fall into,
and trust that you'll always be waiting.

TWENTY-THREE

Stay this close to me, this flush to my skin.
Everything is as it just was.
The traffic beneath my window,
the drone of the ceiling fan.
But now I'm here with you.
I'm full with this soul that speaks to angels,
that knows you completely.
I divest my eyes of their seeing.
I let nothing outside me hold meaning.
I sew myself to this soul.
We enter and leave this world from within.
The miraculous is so subtle, unassuming.
Everything is as it just was.
I'm still alone here in this room.
But the presence of love is now with me.
The door in my heart opens inward.
And heaven rushes up to meet me,
to crowd me with delirious light.

TWENTY-FOUR

Take me to church.
Bring me to my knees.
Make me know you.
Move me from within.
Whisper your vows to me.
Hold what has never been held.
Touch your heart that beats in my chest.
Feel me reach where no one else has been.
Taste this singular kiss that wants you.
Look me in the eyes and don't look away.
Courageously, stay.
Let us blaze in the heat of our symmetry.
Until all that's left of our separateness
is this soul of love that loves through us.

TWENTY-FIVE

This love did not begin when my heart started beating.
It did not begin when I first felt your presence.
Or much later, when I dreamed you.
Or more recently, when I trusted
this presence of love is you.
I loathed math except for that one day.
I had been looking out the window
seeking the words for the vulnerable,
bare arms of the trees reaching skyward.
But then my teacher drew the infinity
symbol on the chalkboard,
chills raced through me and time stood still.
My heart swelled to see it as if a distant
song could suddenly be heard.
X equals Y never made any sense to me.
But I have always known what infinity means.
Not here in these red words.
Not here in these thoughts that form them.
Here in this heart with a love that began long before me.
Here in this momentary body, my cells
hold the paradoxical memory
of what it feels like physically to know that love never dies.
That there is a love that has never left me.
There is a love that will never end.

TWENTY-SIX

I saw you last night standing alone in a cemetery,
    ash and death worn stoically on your face.
    But your eyes were telling me another story,
a warm-blooded heat that consumes without burning,
a searing pain that exacts the dark to birth the light.
    "Only the alpha affords the omega,"
    you said, "the apex, the nadir,
only union's opposite allows the possibility of union."
    I agreed of course but sighed and smiled at you,
    because how many times, beloved,
    will you bring me back to life
without tasting the honey left here on my lips for you?
The path of true love has stripped my ego of its ego.
    What's left of me is tender, pulsing,
    vulnerable and immortal.
    Neruda says that love is "a war of lightening"
    and Gilbert "a hundred vats of honey."
I say love is a heaven found here in our human kiss.

TWENTY-SEVEN

I dance the dance that speaks to you directly.
I am so inside me.
I'm in a place that's beyond mirrors, beyond metaphors,
a place where everything is actually the thing itself.
There is no distance, no dividing.
There is just this sweet intimacy with being real,
with a love so tangible I can hold it in my hands
when I drink tea each morning, when I fold the laundry.
There are many ways of being in a
place, St. Teresa reminds me.
Wherever I am, I never leave this place.
I remain here where you can witness me.
Here where your eyes on my dance lift every last veil.

TWENTY-EIGHT

We all start as mythical creatures.
Land born beings submerged in water.
Our latent lungs waiting patiently in the womb.
Water is the element that carries, that
cleanses, that lets us start new.
I've always been fluent to what water channels.
The pure emotion, the fiery spirit.
I remember the taste of the holy water I gave you.
And what it said to me all that night while you slept.
And I remember what I heard when you baptized me,
months later in the middle of the winter
when everything was still possible, when
every word was a seed we planted.
Water is so holy because it holds, contains.
It is the element that reminds us- when
in the darkness of what might be-
that love is the force that only wants us to receive more life.

TWENTY-NINE

I can feel that you hear me.
Not here in these words,
but in my heart that feels them.
This heart that knows you completely.
This interstice between the worlds,
this is where I found you-
on the same side of the locked door as I am.
And I had been debating about letting you in.
When you came up from behind me,
wrapped your arms around me.
I should have always known.
The resilience in this human heart
is the evidence that it's shared.

THIRTY

My yes for you came from my sacrum,
very earthy, very matter-of-factly.
The body has wisdom thoughts can't touch,
a clarity that feels like a crystal or a stone.
I can think myself away from you.
Emotions can judge and cloud my next move.
My belief in you can doubt itself.
My rational mind has a field day on the subject of you.
But the body, my body never lies.
And it's that my body chose you.
It's that my bones knew your name.
It's that a sweet, essential need for you
hums quietly in my solar plexus.
Even as I sleep,
a pulsing cadence in my root chakra
calls for you in morse code.

THIRTY-ONE

Here sits the holy of holies.
The secret, the diamond, the well.
We are everything and each other.
The light, the dark. The son, the moon.
The mother, the sky. The father, the earth,
the orb of light that orbits us.
The dawn, the daughter,
the fixed presence that forgives us.
We are everything and each other.
We can only heal if we see together
the red thread looped around the back of our hearts.
No matter how separate we think we are,
no worldly knife or hardened words can break it.
No amount of our own humanity can untether it.
We can't undo what we didn't create.
And so love is a bond that can't be unmade.

THIRTY-TWO

What if we met deep in the earth of our unconscious.
And what if we wrestle there
even in our sleep.
What if we knew the hieros gamos
not from thoughts or theories
but from the spirit suddenly here in our sinews.
What if we are meant to resurrect that ancient ritual
of what becoming one is meant to be.
Not a subtraction or reduction
but a sacred geometry.
What if the vesica piscis is the truest wedding portrait-
the untouchable topography of an inner union
where my humanity eclipses your divinity.
Where the infinite forms an egg.
Where endless possibility swells inside me.
Where my yes has made you
bone of my bones and flesh of my flesh.
Where I am yours, beloved, and you are mine.

THIRTY-THREE

I vow to never forget: I am you.
I vow to recognize: you're right here,
in the cadence of my breath,
in the dull quiet ache, of wanting only more of you.
I vow to let our union guide me.
Not just your heaven, but also my earth.
Not just your strength, but also my weakness.
I vow to be a presence of love made more
powerful because imperfect, faltering.
Made more powerful because my broken
spaces are where you enter me.
I vow to be nothing more than I am.
This singular chance to marry your love to my humanity.

THIRTY-FOUR

Nothing begins that hasn't always existed.
I was awake inside a dream.
My task was to make the cross out of three small sticks.
The first two formed the cross I knew.
The one that scared me as a little girl-
thinking it meant exclusion, judgment.
Now, it meant heaven meeting earth,
life meeting death, above meeting below.
I held the third stick and suddenly saw its place.
To pierce the point where all opposites intersect.
So that love is no longer two-dimensional.
So that no story of love has ever ended.
So that love is what happens on this axis.
Not transcendence, but immanence.
So that love is what we bring into existence.
Love is what will always resurrect.

THIRTY-FIVE

This is what consummation looks like:
A melting inward, a subtle surrender, that
never blurs your body and mine,
but sustains our separateness as we enter each other;
as my love beheads your ego;
and as your presence makes molten
honey of my bloodstream.
This is what consummation looks like:
a courageous sight, a differentiated union;
where you remain you and I remain my own.
So that the holy third rises inside us,
so that we give birth to the divine.
No sacrifice, no settling. No compromise, or negotiating.
This is what consummation looks like:
a mutual submission, a trusted memory,
that we are in each other.
And so we are now made more boldly this
breath, more fiercely this soul.

THIRTY-SIX

I am so surrendered, so entirely claimed,
my soul is crowned with sovereignty.
I am so vulnerable, I am inviolable.
I am so humbled, I am exalted.
I am so weak, I am strength.
I am so still, and silent, I hear everything.
I am so much alone, and on my own,
the whole world comforts me.
I am so empty, and vessel-like, the universe fits inside me.
I am so infinitesimally small, there's
nothing my heart cannot hold.
I am so fragile, and delicate, there's
nothing left of me to break.
I am so much the love that you are, beloved,
that there's no place this love cannot reach.

THIRTY-SEVEN

I am the essence of amber, jasmine, geranium.
I am the slow ardent ache here in your heart.
I am the quiet, restless impulse that moves you toward me.
I am the simple grains of sand the mollusk makes the pearl.
I am the staid, high-walls that make the verdant garden.
I am the elemental mineral in the dark
that pressure makes the diamond.
I am the humble power that has no use of force.
I am the pure existence that always follows pleasure.
I am the tender reception of every possible sensation.
I am the beauty that remains after death fades.
I am the dove, the bird that invariably rises.
I am the skull, the candle with its ceaseless flame.
I am the awe that swells in you when I'm remembered.
I am the love that floods you, that overwhelms all fear.
I am the soul who has desired you infinitely.
I am the voice of your heart, beloved, and
you have known me completely.

THIRTY-EIGHT

It's that what is our inside is our outside.
And what is above is also below.
It's that the bride is not the bride.
And the groom is foremost that ancient masculine
that stands hand in hand with the sacred feminine
in a wedding chamber that can only be sensed.
It's that their union restores a holy worth to all sexes.
It's that we are not male or female.
We are either married to the soul or still searching.
It's that we either see or don't see
that we can never harm the other without
equally harming ourselves.
Deep, in those unfathomable depths inside us
this inward marriage binds us in an infinite love.
It's that this is the source of my courage, beloved.
This love is what lets me see every love as beloved to me.

THIRTY-NINE

This is the secret that everyone knows.
Love- true love- is what can never leave.
I've searched everywhere for you.
I've died small deaths to find you.
I've crossed seas in the hopes of seeing your face.
I've broken my heart against other loves wanting to feel you.
I've made my life about this seeking, this one-day-finding.
So a new life begins now, beloved.
Because all this time, you were with me.
All this time you were the desire I had to find you.
I can see the radiant white bridge that's inside my heart.
I can see that you have been standing there
waiting for me to come join you.
I was never alone and never without you.
A new life begins today, the life spent with you.
This is the secret that everyone knows.
Love- true love- is what can never leave.
And this beloved is what I have become for you.

FORTY

Beloved.
The end will be
where the beginning is.
Heart to heart speaks directly.
The two worlds were always one.
Your voice is here inside this red ink.
Your presence is here woven in this body.
Your love surges up from behind these eyes.
And there's no place your love does not reach.
Your love, beloved, has made me fully human.
What's eternal now lives in this transient heart.
So wherever I go now, beloved, I go with you.
We're tethered together with unspeakable joy.
We will share what ears have not heard.
And what eyes have not ever seen.
With our love, heaven is here,
And in our words, angels
will kiss the earth.
Beloved.

:::A BENEDICTION:::

Beloved

Love lives in a time outside of time.
It has no morals, no code of ethics to stand by.
It pushes us beyond what was possible before.
It forces us to meet with those aspects of our
being we've been too afraid to see.
It wants to witness what has been alone in us.
It wants us to reveal all that we are, especially
where we are broken and human.
It wants us to let it enter those places in
us we've long since boarded up.
Love wants us to realize that we are love.
By any means possible, at any point in our lives,
and whether through a stray pet or a soul
mate found, love comes unbidden.
Love wrecks the whole of who we were.
Love asks everything of us so we can be
the one we've come here for.

Manufactured by Amazon.ca
Bolton, ON

26674632R00055